FJH SOLOS ARE THEIR BEST!

BOOK 6
Late Intermediate

CONTENTS

from Lyric Scenes

Shadows in the Snow

Mary Leaf

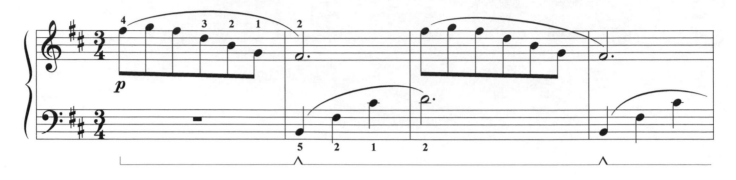

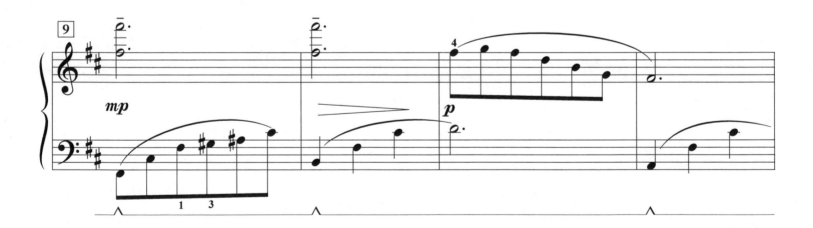

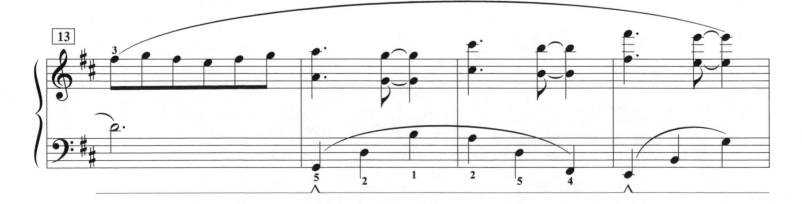

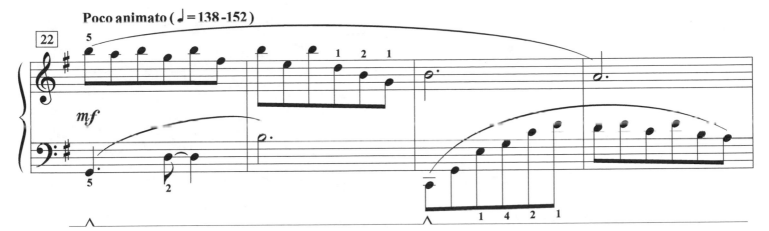

Poco animato (♩ = 138 -152)

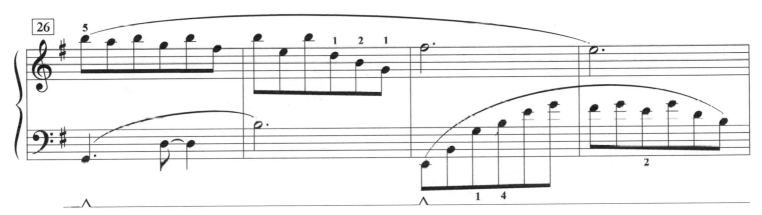

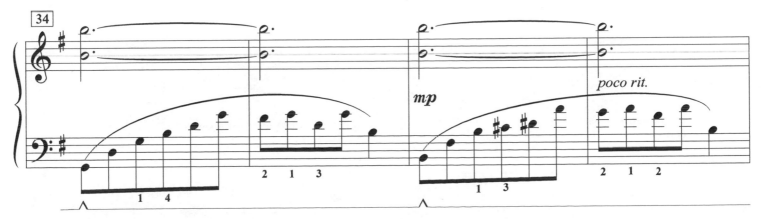

4

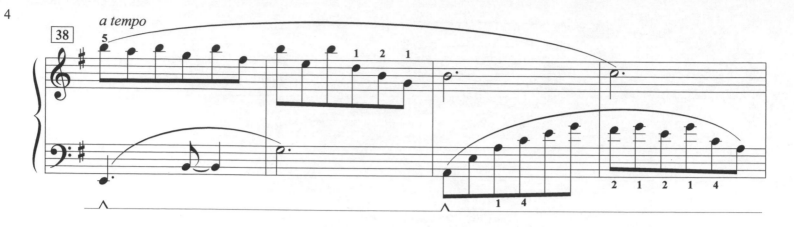

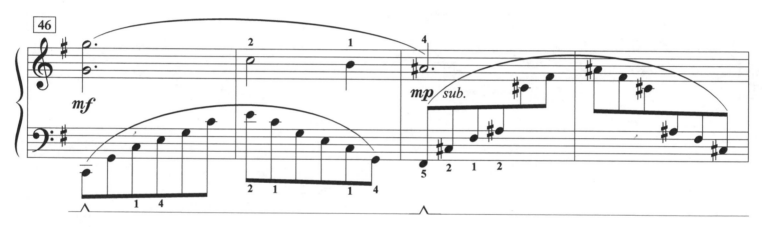

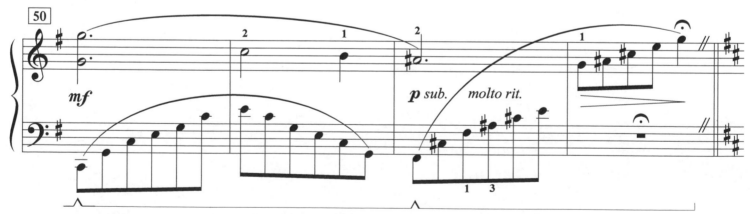

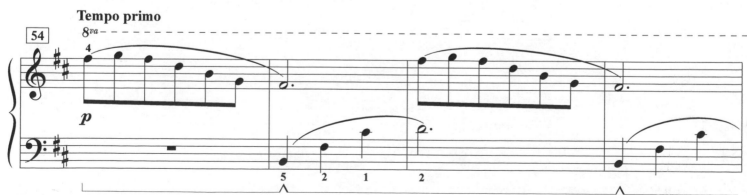

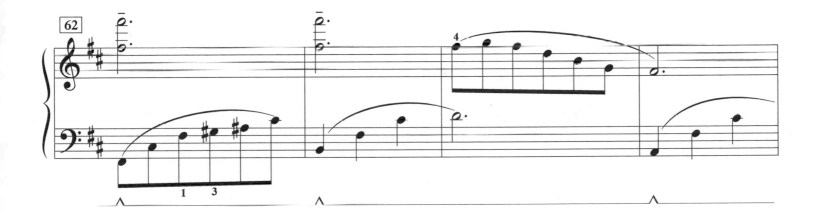

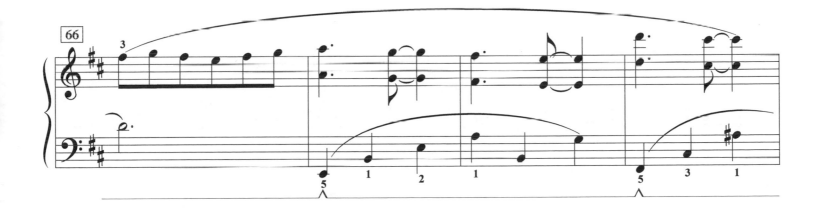

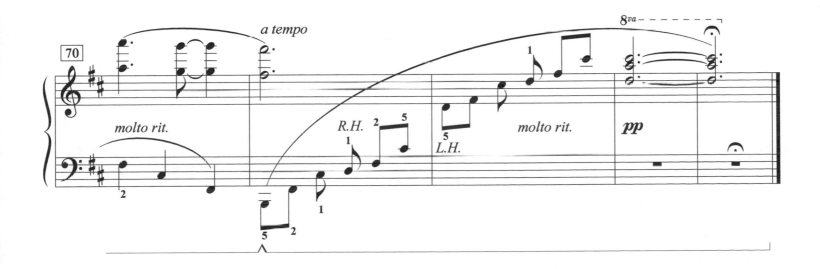

Summer Rain

Listen for the light patter of rain when you play this piece.

Christopher Goldston

Expressively; with persistence (♩ = ca. 104)

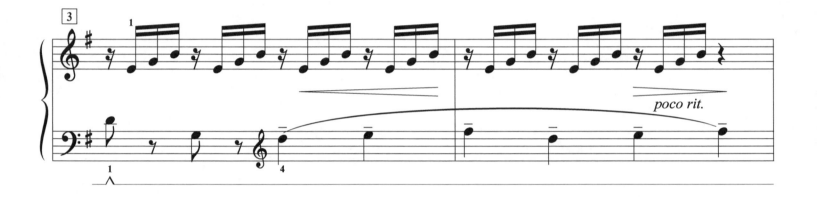

8

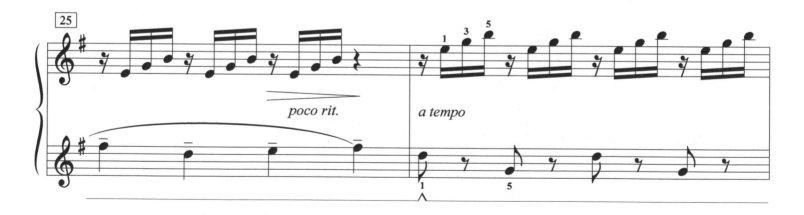

for Roberto and Beti Velert

Nocturne

(Nightfall in Tossa de Mar)

Martín Cuéllar

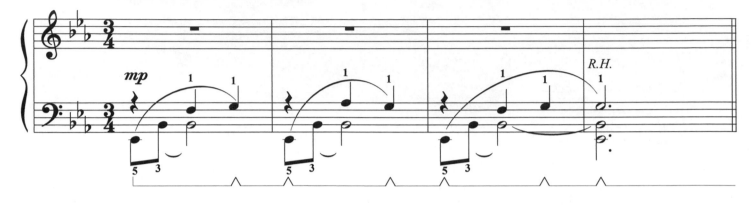

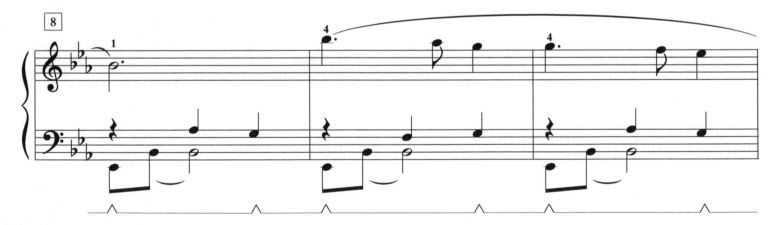

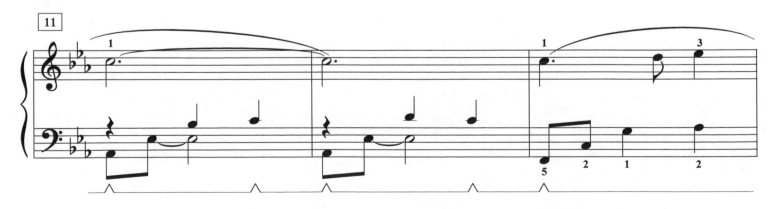

FJH2295

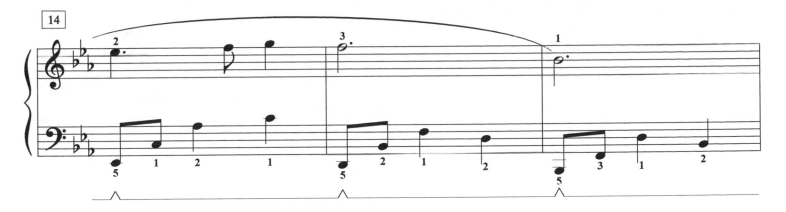

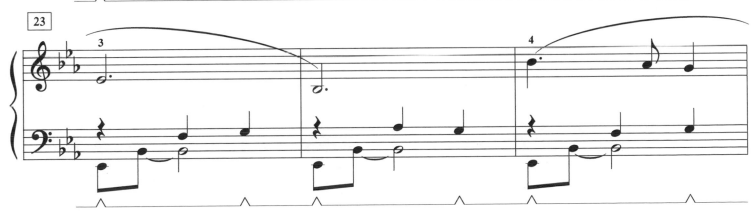

12

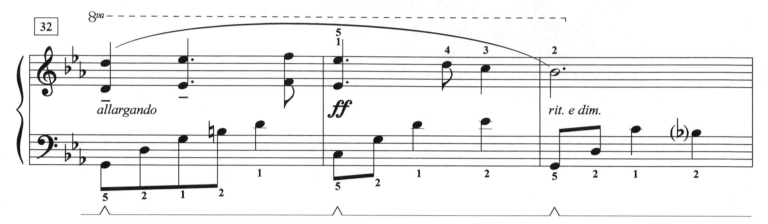

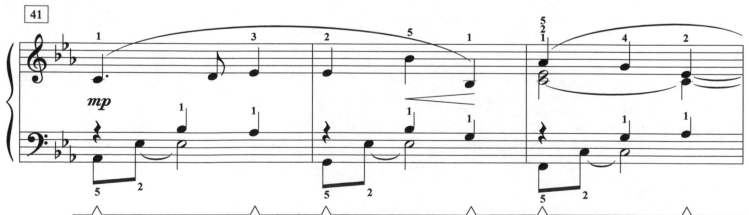

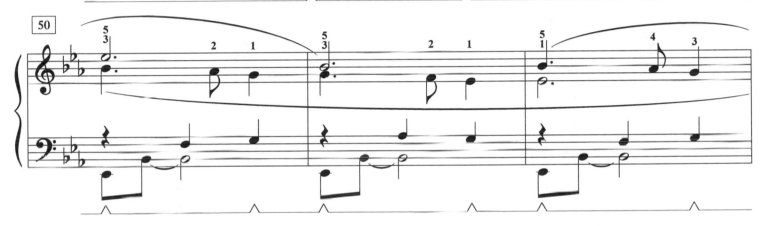

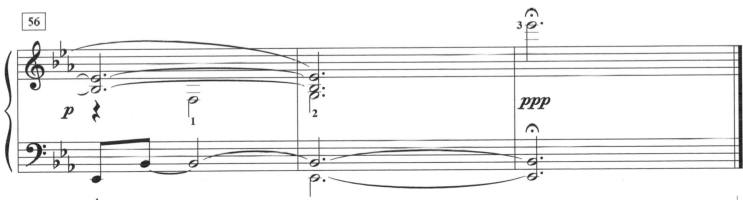

Toccata Andaluza

from In Style! Book 3

Timothy Brown

Driving; insistent (♩ = ca. 160)

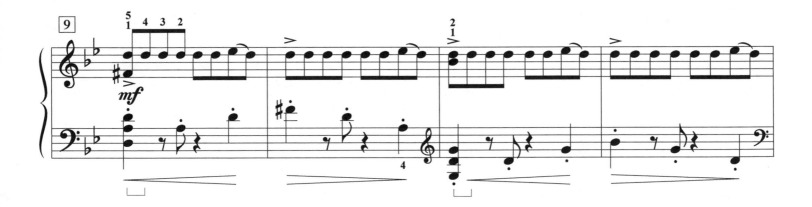

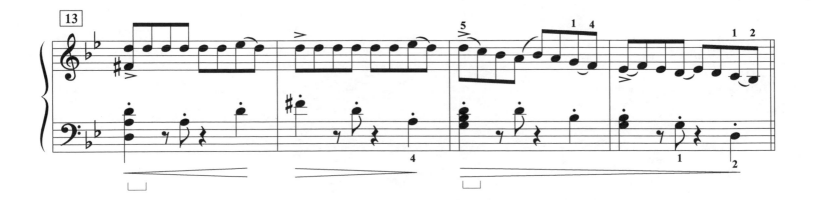

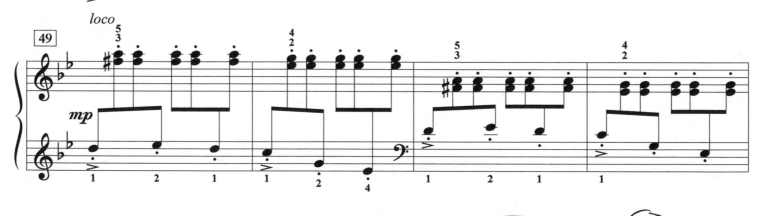

for Giselda Renelda

Wizard Fantasy

Mary Leaf

Frenzied, but whimsical (♩ = 100-108)

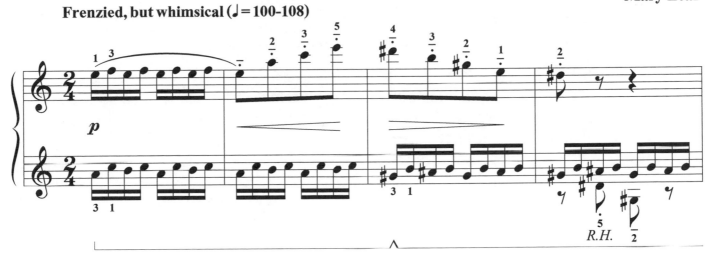

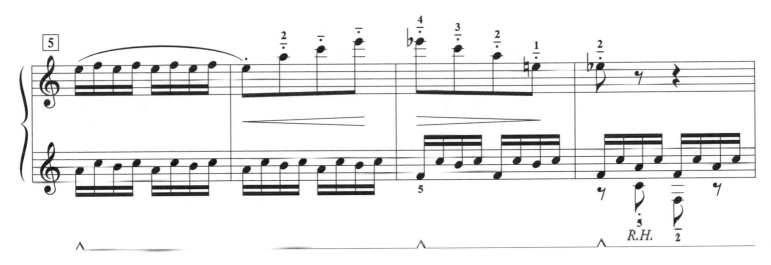

FJH2295

18

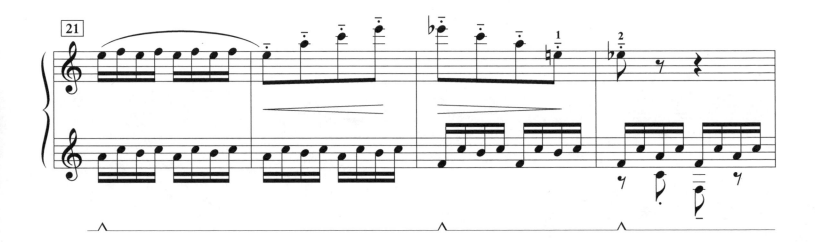

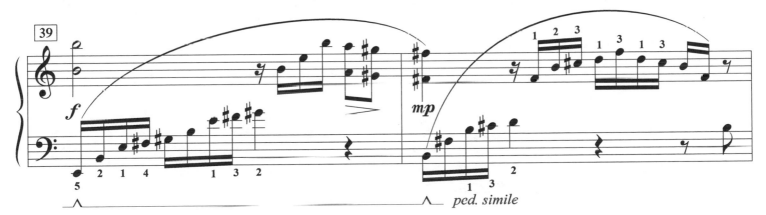

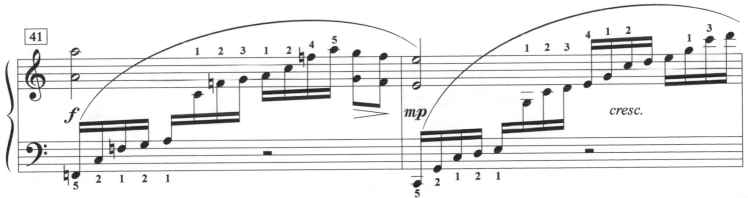

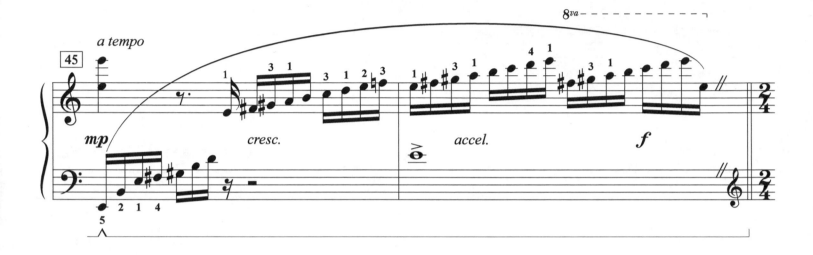

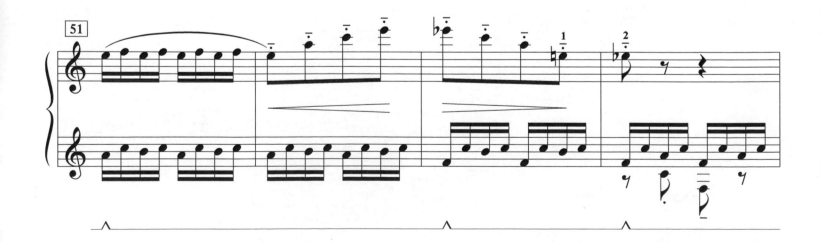

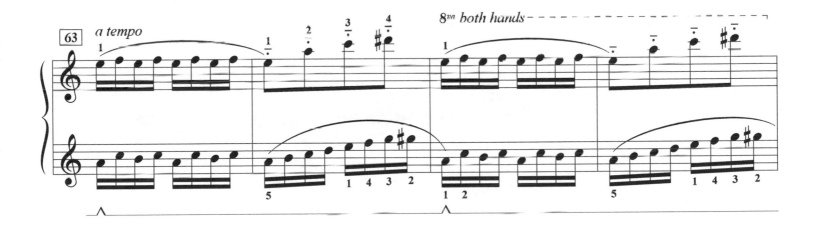

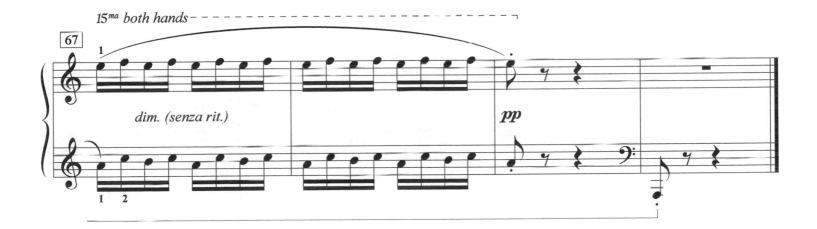

for the Pittsburgh Piano Teachers Association

Round 'Em Up

from An American Sonatina

Timothy Brown

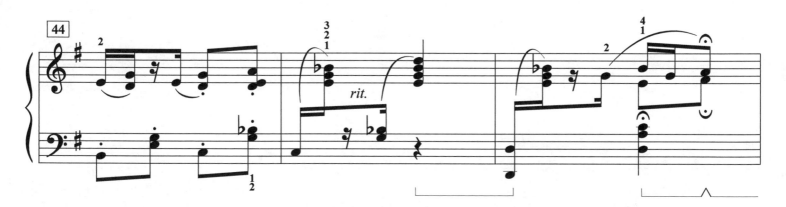

Nouvelle Étude

Edwin McLean

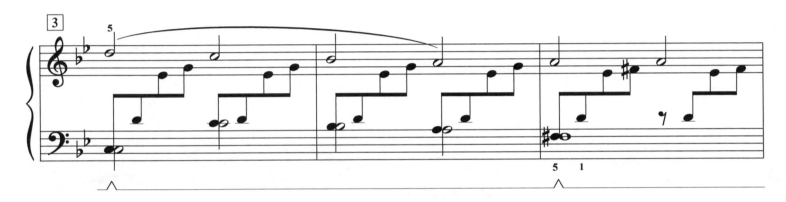

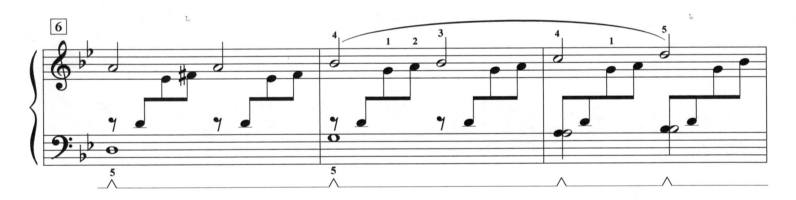

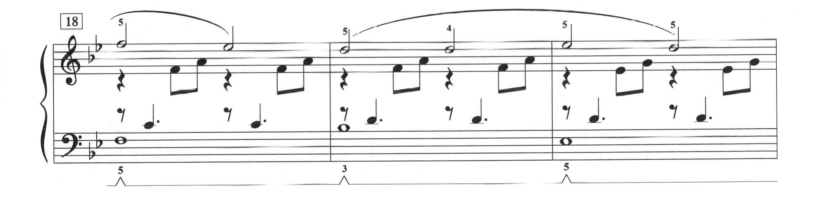

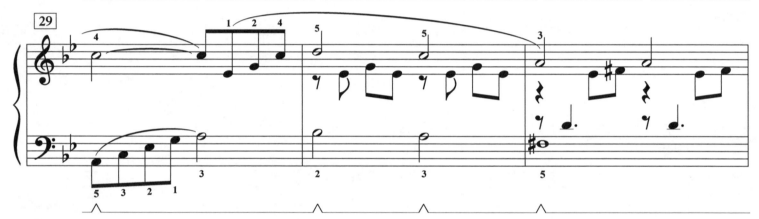

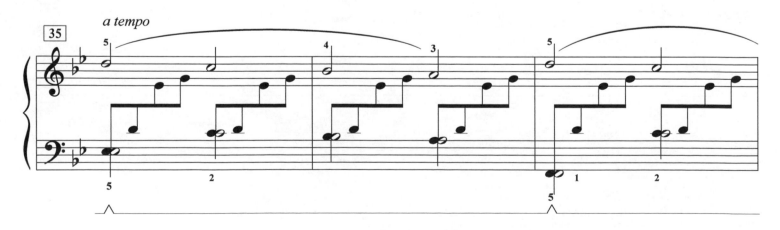

commissioned for the 20th anniversary of the Jordan River Chapter of the
Utah Music Teachers Association

Oquirrh Mountains Shining

The Oquirrh Mountains rise above the western Salt Lake Valley, not far from where I grew up.
The name "Oquirrh" (pronounced "OAK-er") comes from the Ute word for "shining" mountains.

Kevin Olson

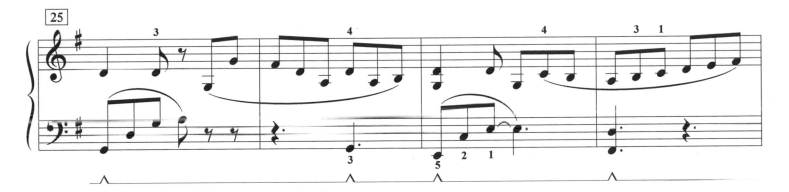

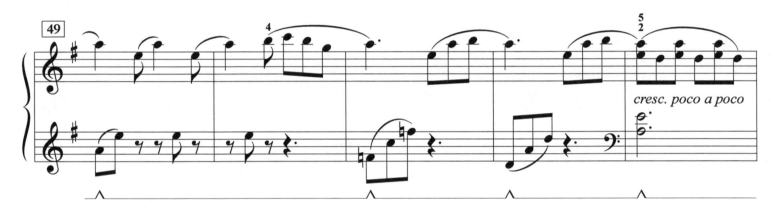

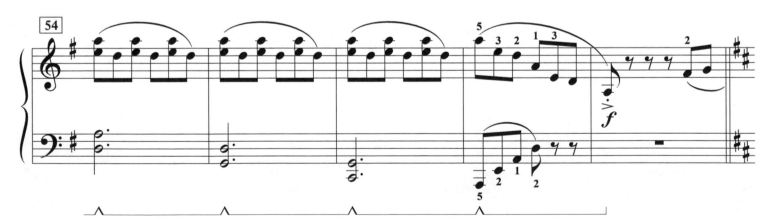

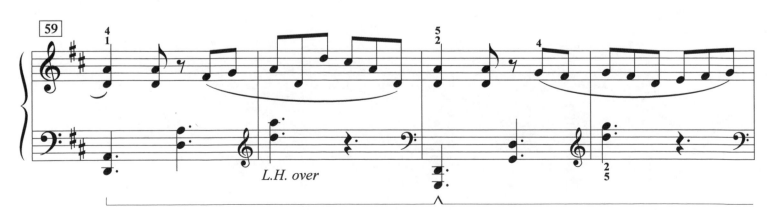

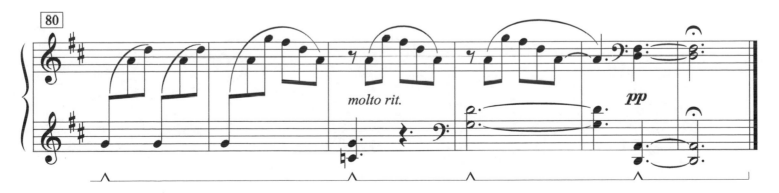

Son cubano

from ¡Fiesta!

Lee Evans

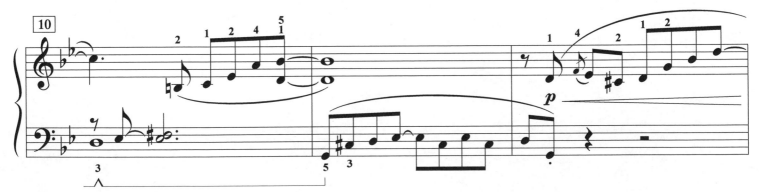

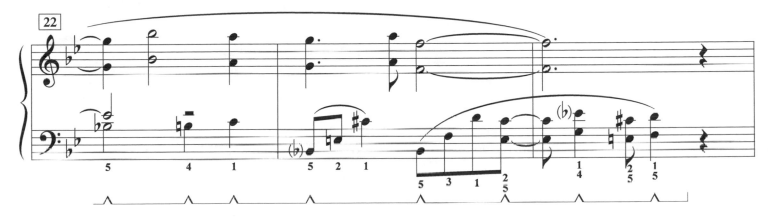

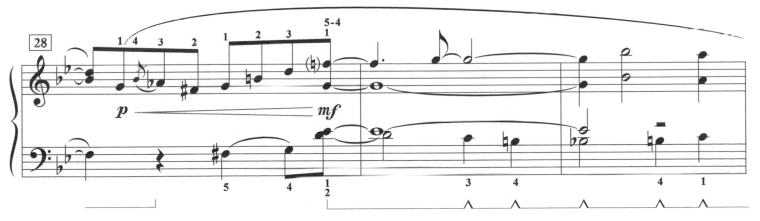

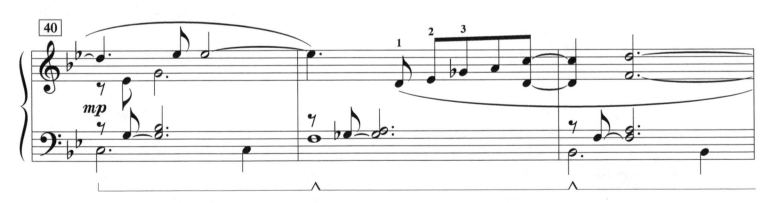

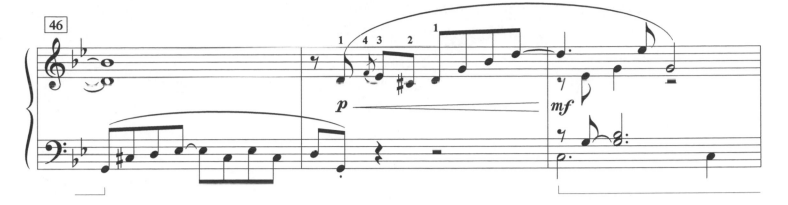

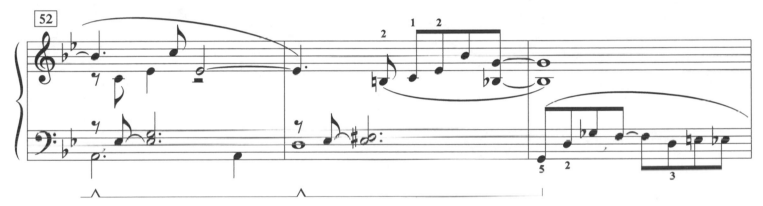

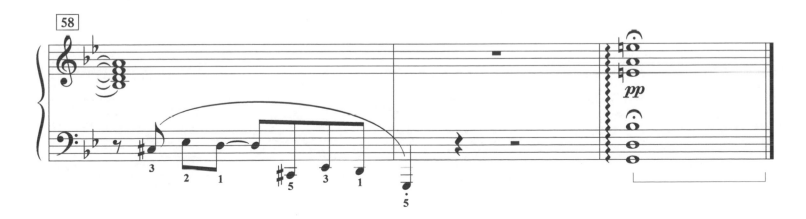

to the teachers and students of the Pikes Peak Music Teachers Association

Tribute to Pikes Peak

Melody Bober

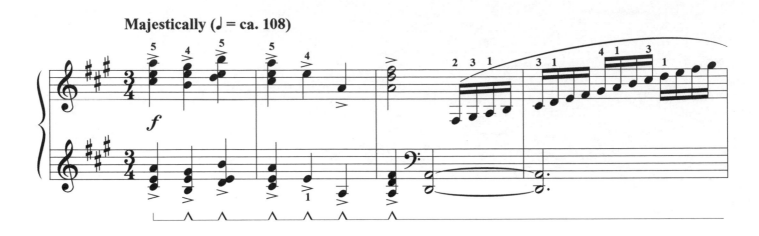

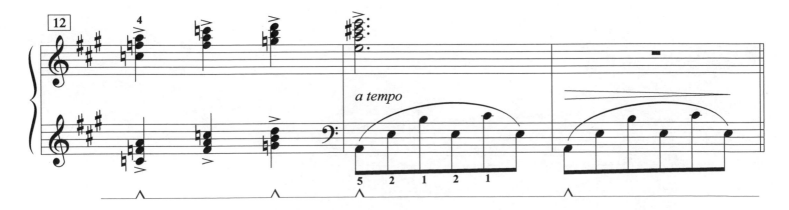

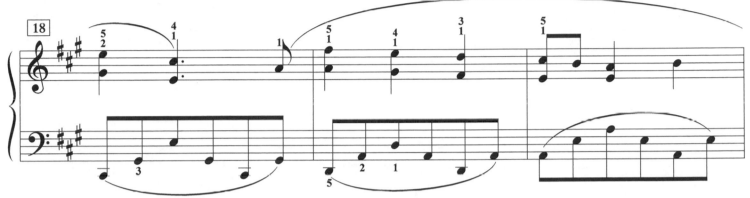

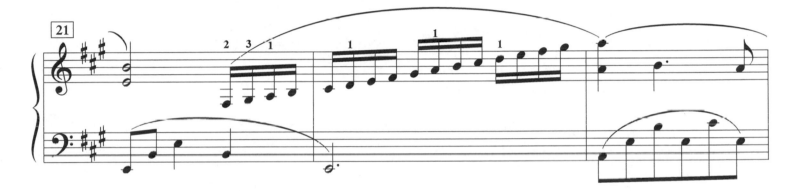

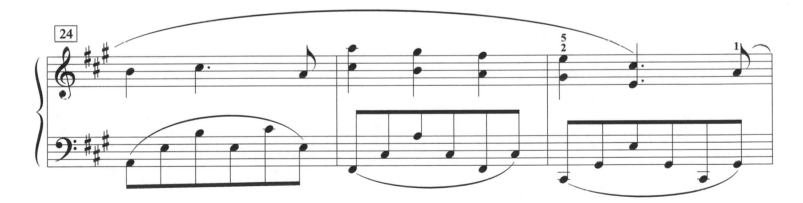

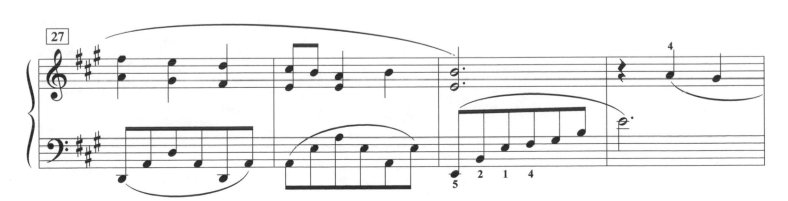

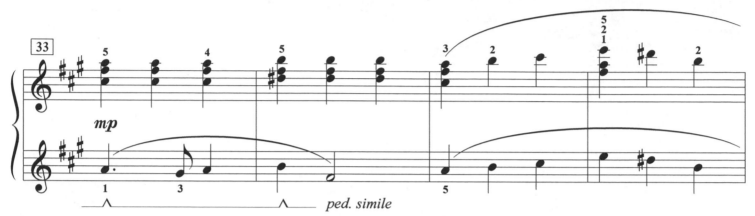

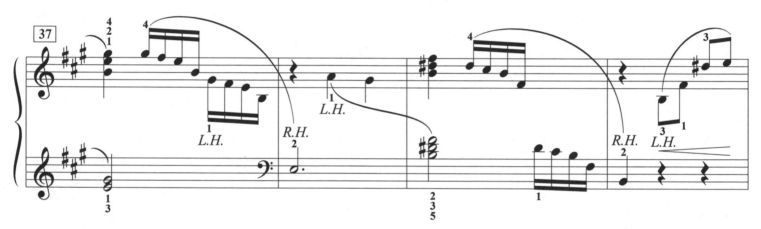

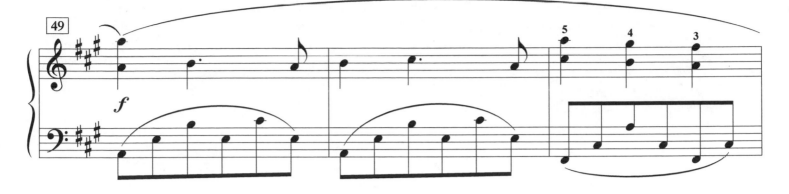

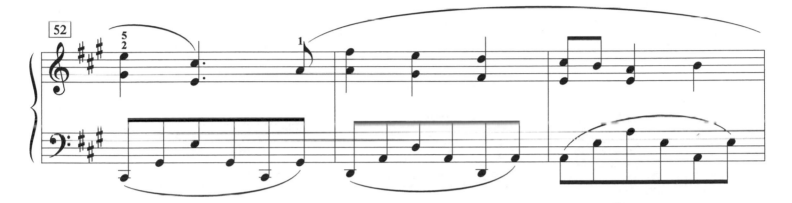

A little slower (♩ = ca. 92)

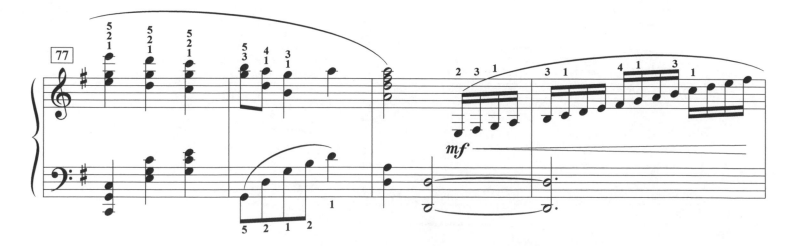

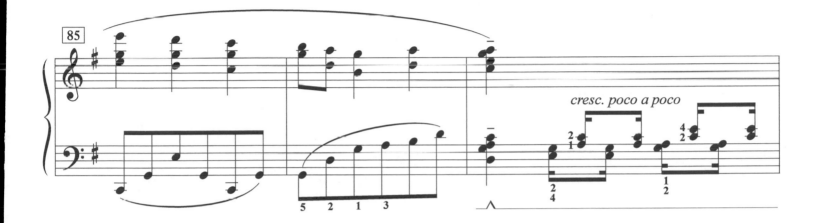

dedicated to the Pikes Peak Music Teachers Association

Front Range

Front Range is the name given to the majestic mountain range that overlooks Denver and Colorado Springs

Kevin Olson

Flowing; with energy (♩. = ca. 72)

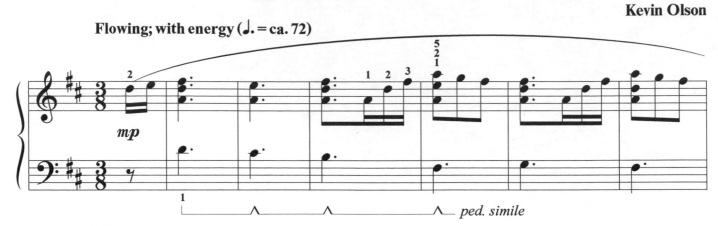

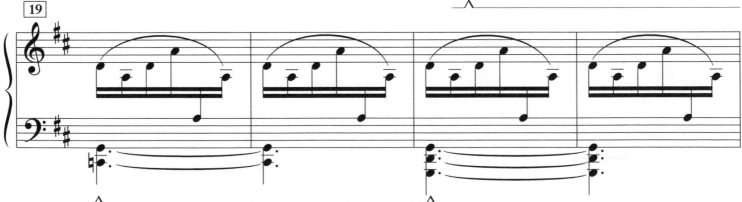

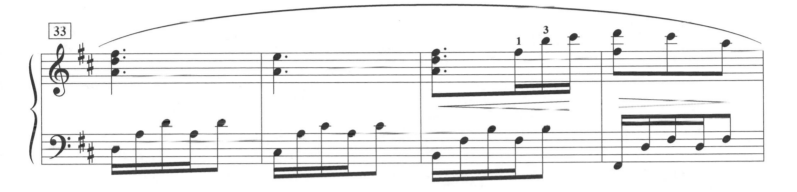

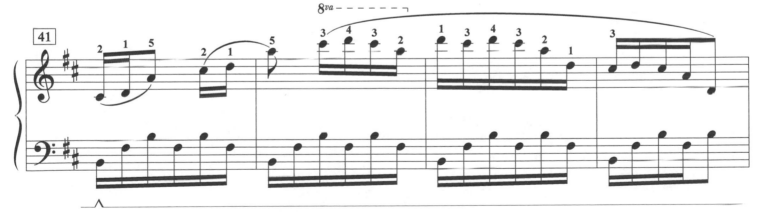

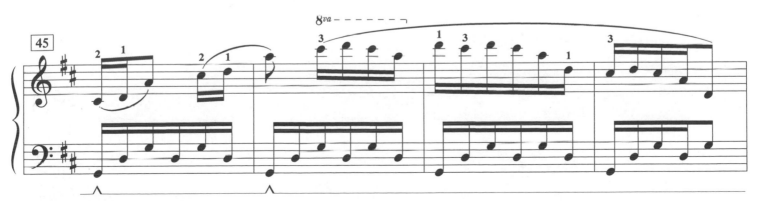

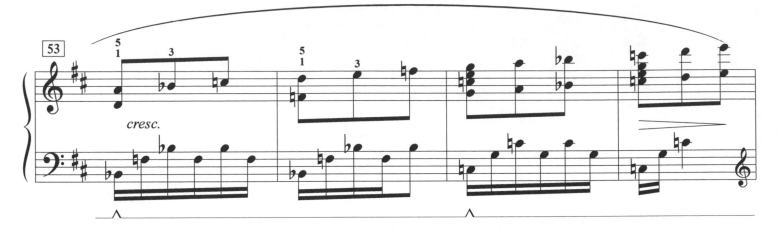

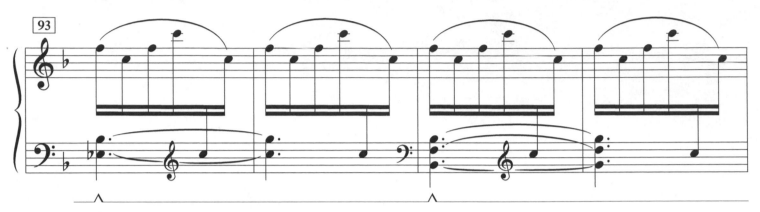

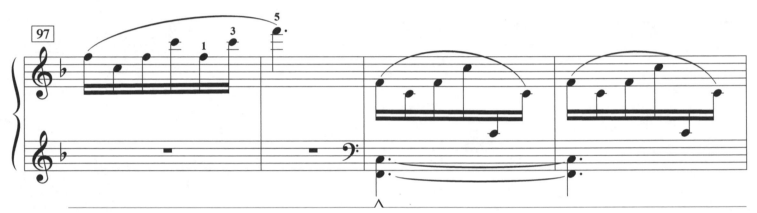

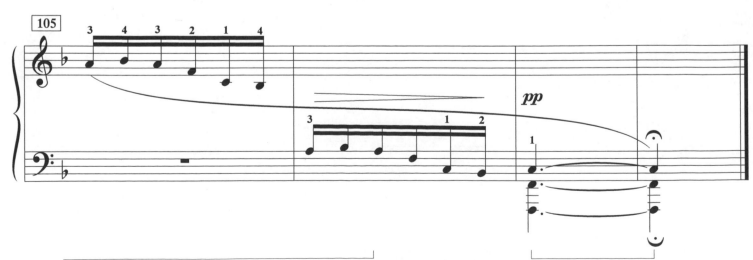